DIGEST AND REVISION OF STRYKER'S
OFFICERS AND MEN OF NEW JERSEY
IN THE REVOLUTIONARY WAR
WHO WERE ELIGIBLE TO MEMBERSHIP IN

THE SOCIETY OF THE
CINCINNATI

I0099331

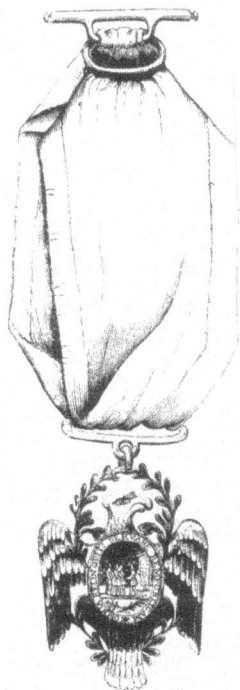

James Wall Schureman Campbell

HERITAGE BOOKS
2011

HERITAGE BOOKS

AN IMPRINT OF HERITAGE BOOKS, INC.

Books, CDs, and more—Worldwide

For our listing of thousands of titles see our website
at
www.HeritageBooks.com

A Facsimile Reprint
Published 2011 by
HERITAGE BOOKS, INC.
Publishing Division
100 Railroad Ave. #104
Westminster, Maryland 21157

— Publisher's Notice —
In reprints such as this, it is often not possible to remove blemishes from
the original. We feel the contents of this book warrant its reissue despite
these blemishes and hope you will agree and read it with pleasure.

International Standard Book Numbers
Paperbound: 978-1-55613-033-5
Clothbound: 978-0-7884-8775-0

OFFICERS OF

The Society of the Cincinnati in the State of New Jersey

——: 1911 :——

PRESIDENT

James Wall Schureman Campbell
Freehold, N. J.

VICE-PRESIDENT

William Pennington
800 Broad Street, Newark, N. J.

SECRETARY

Lewis Dunham Boggs
23 Warren Street, New York City

TREASURER

William McKnight Reckless
Freehold, N. J.

ASSISTANT SECRETARY

Ulric Dahlgren
Princeton, N. J.

ASSISTANT TREASURER

Paul Augustine Hendry
1713 Montgomery Ave., Philadelphia, Pa.

Roster of the New Jersey Officers of the Continental Line, Army of the Revolution, Who Were Eligible to Membership in the Society of the Cincinnati

BRIGADIER GENERALS.

* || Dayton, Elias. (Original member.) Colonel, Third Battalion, First Establishment, February 9th, 1776; Colonel, Third Battalion, Second Establishment, November 28th, 1776; Colonel, Third Regiment; Brigadier General, Continental Army, January 7th, 1783; discharged at the close of the war; took part in all the battles in which the Continental Line of New Jersey was engaged; commanded the Jersey Brigade after the resignation of Brigadier General Maxwell; also Colonel of militia.

Maxwell, William. Colonel, Second Battalion, First Establishment, November 8th, 1775; Brigadier General, Continental Army, October 23d, 1776; resigned July 25th, 1780; commanded the "Jersey Line" during his entire term of service as a general officer, and took an active part in every battle in which his brigade distinguished itself.

COLONELS.

Forman, David. (Original member.) Colonel, "Forman's Regiment," Continental Army; also Brigadier General, militia.

* Ogden, Matthias. (Original member.) Lieutenant Colonel, First Battalion, First Establishment, March 7th, 1776; Lieutenant Colonel, First Battalion, Second Establishment, November 28th, 1776; Colonel, ditto, January 1st, 1777; Colonel, First Regiment; taken prisoner November 4th, 1780; granted leave of absence by Congress April 21st, 1783, to visit Europe; discharged at the close of the war.

* Shreve, Israel. (Original member.) Lieutenant Colonel, Second Battalion, First Establishment, November 8th, 1775; Colonel, Second Battalion, Second Establishment, November 28th, 1776; Colonel, Second Regiment; discharged at the close of the war.

* Spencer, Oliver. (Original member.) Colonel, "Spencer's Regiment," Continental Army, January 15th, 1777; discharged at the close of the war; also Colonel, militia.

White, Anthony Walton. (Original member, State of New York transferred to New Jersey.) Major and Aid-de-Camp to General Washington, October, 1775; Lieutenant Colonel, Third Battalion, First Establishment, February 9th, 1776; Lieutenant Colonel, Fourth Regiment, Light Dragoons, Continental Army, February 13th, 1777; Lieutenant Colonel Commandant, First Regiment, ditto, December 10th, 1779; Colonel, ditto, February 16th, 1780, and ordered to command all cavalry in Southern Army.

Winds, William. Lieutenant Colonel, First Battalion, First Establishment, November 7th, 1775; Colonel, ditto, March 7th, 1776; discharged with battalion; Brigadier General, militia, March 4th, 1777.

LIEUTENANT COLONELS.

Brearley, David. (Original member.) Lieutenant Colonel, Fourth Battalion, Second Establishment, November 28th, 1776; Lieutenant Colonel, First Regiment, to date January 1st, 1777; resigned March 17th, 1780, to accept office of Chief Justice of the State; also Colonel, militia.

Burr, Aaron. (Original member, State of New York.)

Lieutenant Colonel and Aid-de-Camp, staff of Major General Israel Putnam.

Conway, John. (Original member.) Captain, First Battalion, First Establishment, November 21st, 1775; Captain, First Battalion, Second Establishment, November 29th, 1776; Major, Fourth Battalion, Second Establishment, October 29th, 1777; Major, Third Regiment; Lieutenant Colonel, First Regiment, to date March 17th, 1780; wounded at the battle of Germantown; discharged at the close of the war.

*Cumming, John N. (Original member.) First Lieutenant, Captain Howell's company, Second Battalion, First Establishment, November 29th, 1775; First Lieutenant, Captain Lawrie's company, Second Battalion, Second Establishment, November 29th, 1776; Captain, Second Battalion, ditto, to date November 30th, 1776; Captain, Second Regiment; Major, First Regiment, to date April 16th, 1780; Lieutenant Colonel, Second Regiment, December 29th, 1781; Lieutenant Colonel Commandant, Third Regiment, February 11th, 1783; discharged at the close of the war.

D'Hart, William. Major, First Battalion, First Establishment, November 7th, 1775; Major, First Battalion, Second Establishment, November 28th, 1776; Lieutenant Colonel, ditto, January 1st, 1777; Lieutenant Colonel, Second Regiment, September 26th, 1780; resigned.

*Forman, Jonathan. (Original member.) Captain, Fourth Battalion, Second Establishment; November 23d, 1776; Captain, First Regiment, September 26th, 1780; Major, Third Regiment, November 20th, 1781; Lieutenant Colonel, Second Regiment, February 11th, 1783; discharged at the close of the war; also Captain, militia.

Lindsley, Eleazer. Lieutenant Colonel, "Spencer's Regiment," Continental Army; resigned; also Lieutenant Colonel, militia; Second Major, "Eastern Battalion" Morris, January 13th, 1776; Lieutenant Colonel, ditto; also Lieutenant Colonel, Continental Army.

Rhea, David. Major, Second Battalion, First Establishment, November 8th, 1775; Lieutenant Colonel, Second Battalion, Second Establishment; November 28th, 1776; retired September 26th, 1780.

Smith, William. Lieutenant Colonel, "Spencer's Regiment," Continental Army.

MAJORS.

Barber, William. Ensign, Third Battalion, First Establishment, October 29th, 1776; Ensign, Captain Ross's company, Third Battalion, Second Establishment, November 29th, 1776; resigned; afterwards Lieutenant and Aid-de-Camp to Brigadier General William Maxwell, January 1st, 1777; Captain, ditto, April 14th, 1777; Major, ditto, May 7th, 1778; Major and Aid-de-Camp to Major General Lord Stirling, October, 1778; wounded at the siege of Yorktown; discharged at the close of the war.

Bloomfield, Joseph. (Original member.) Captain, Third Battalion, First Establishment, February 9th, 1776; Major, Third Battalion, Second Establishment; November 28th, 1776; resigned October 29th, 1778, to accept civil office; was Judge Advocate Northern Army, November, 1776.

* Bowman, Nathaniel. (Original member.) Second Lieutenant, Captain Faulkner's company, Second Battalion, First Establishment, November 13th, 1775; First Lieutenant, Captain Dillon's company, ditto, May 10th, 1776; First Lieutenant, Captain Anderson's company, Second Battalion, Second Establishment, November 29th, 1776; First Lieutenant, Captain Dillon's company, ditto, February 5th, 1777; Captain, Second Battalion, ditto, September 11th, 1777; Captain, Second Regiment, September 26th, 1780; Major by brevet; Major, Third Regiment, February 11th, 1783; discharged at the close of the war.

* ‡ Bruen, Jeremiah. (Original member. Dropped from Rolls, 1806.) Captain, "Baldwin's Regiment of Artificers," Continental Army, March 2d, 1777; Major, ditto, November 12th, 1779.

Burnet, Ichabod. (Original member State of Georgia.) Major and Aid-de-Camp, Continental Army, January 9th, 1778.

* Burrowes, John. (Original member.) Captain, "For-

man's Regiment," Continental Army; Captain, "Spencer's Regiment," Continental Army, January 1st, 1777; Major, ditto, July 22d, 1779; discharged at the close of the war.

* **Cox, Richard.** (Original member.) Second Lieutenant, Captain Ross's company, Third Battalion, First Establishment, February 9th, 1776; First Lieutenant, ditto, October 29th, 1776; First Lieutenant, Captain Ross's company, Third Battalion, Second Establishment, November 29th, 1776; Captain, ditto, January 1st, 1777; Captain, Third Regiment, September 23d, 1780; Captain, First Regiment; Brigade Major to Brigadier General William Maxwell; Major, Second Regiment, January 6th, 1783; discharged at the close of the war.

Doughty, John. (Original member State of New York, transferred to New Jersey, 1793.) Captain, Third Battalion, Second Establishment, November 29th, 1776; Major, Third Battalion, ditto; resigned; Captain Lieutenant, Eastern Artillery Company State Troops, May 9th, 1776; Captain, Second Continental Regiment Artillery, January 1st, 1777; Aid-de-Camp to Major-General Schuyler, 1777; Colonel and Aid-de-Camp to the Commander-in-Chief, etc., etc.

Hollinshead, John. (Original member.) First Lieutenant, Captain Lawrie's company, Second Battalion, First Establishment, November 27th, 1775; First Lieutenant, Captain Brearley's company, Second Battalion, Second Establishment, November 29th, 1776; Captain, Second Battalion, ditto, February 5th, 1777; Captain, Second Regiment; Major, Third Regiment, to date July 5th, 1779; resigned November 20th, 1781.

Howell, Richard. (Original member.) Captain, Second Battalion, First Establishment, November 29th, 1775; Brigade Major, September 4th, 1776; Major, Second Battalion, Second Establishment, November 28th, 1776; Major, Second Regiment, resigned, to date April 7th, 1779.

* **Ogden, Aaron.** (Original member.) Paymaster, First Battalion, First Establishment, December 8th, 1775; Paymaster, First Battalion, Second Establishment, February 1st, 1777; resigned as Paymaster April 1st, 1778; Captain-Lieutenant, First Regiment; Captain, ditto, to date February 2d, 1779;

Brigade Major and Inspector and Aid-de-Camp to Brigadier General William Maxwell, April 1st, 1778; discharged at the close of the war.

Polhemus, John. (Original member. Dropped from Rolls 1793.) Captain, First Battalion, First Establishment, November 22d, 1775; Captain, First Battalion, Second Establishment, November 29th, 1776; Major, ditto; retired September 26th, 1780.

* Reading, Samuel. (Original member.) First Lieutenant, Captain Stout's company, Second Battalion, First Establishment, December 18th, 1775; taken prisoner at Three Rivers, June 8th, 1776; Captain, Second Battalion, Second Establishment, February 5th, 1777; Captain, Second Regiment, to date January 1st, 1777; Major, First Regiment, December 29th, 1781; discharged at the close of the war.

Ross, John. (Original member.) Captain, Third Battalion, First Establishment, February 9th, 1776; Captain, Third Battalion, Second Establishment, November 29th, 1776; Captain, Third Regiment; Major, Second Regiment, to date April 7th, 1779; promoted Brigade Major and Inspector, Jersey Brigade; discharged at the close of the war; also Lieutenant Colonel, militia.

ADJUTANTS.

* Halsey, Luther. (Original member.) Serjeant, Second Battalion, First Establishment; Adjutant, Second Battalion, Second Establishment, November 28th, 1776; Lieutenant and Adjutant, Second Regiment, to date November 9th, 1777; discharged at the close of the war; Captain by brevet.

King, Joseph. Adjutant, Fourth Battalion, Second Establishment, November 28th, 1776; wounded and taken prisoner, June 26th, 1777, at Short Hills, Essex county, New Jersey; retired September 26th, 1780; afterwards Paymaster, Continental Army; also Adjutant, militia.

Shippard, Samuel. Adjutant, Third Battalion, First Establishment, February 9th, 1776; Adjutant, Third Battalion, Second Establishment, November 28th, 1776; Lieutenant and

Adjutant, Third Regiment, to date November 12th, 1777; Lieutenant, First Regiment; resigned to date July 7th, 1780.

*Whitlock, Ephraim. (Original member.) Ensign, Fourth Battalion, Second Establishment, November 28th, 1776; Ensign, Captain Forman's company, ditto, February 17th, 1777; Second Lieutenant, ditto; First Lieutenant, ditto, November 23d, 1777; Lieutenant, First Regiment, to date August 1st, 1779; Lieutenant and Adjutant, ditto; discharged at the close of the war; Captain by brevet; also Ensign, militia.

QUARTERMASTERS.

Clark, Joseph. Quartermaster, staff of Major General Adam Stephens.

Darby, Ephraim. (Original member.) Private, Fourth Battalion, Second Establishment; Quartermaster, ditto, February 17th, 1777; Lieutenant and Quartermaster, Third Regiment, to date November 12th, 1777; Lieutenant, First Regiment; discharged at the close of the war; Captain by brevet; also Captain, militia.

Douglass, Ephraim. Quartermaster, staff of Major General Lord Stirling; taken prisoner at Bushwick, Long Island, August 27th, 1776.

Ford, Chilleon. (Original member.) Second Lieutenant, "Lamb's Artillery," (Second Regiment Artillery), Continental Army, April 10th, 1777; Quartermaster, ditto, August 1st, 1779.

Lott, Peter. Ensign, First Battalion, Second Establishment; Second Lieutenant, ditto; Ensign and Quartermaster, First Regiment; Lieutenant and Quartermaster, ditto, to date February 25th, 1778; resigned, to date March 27th, 1780.

McEwen, John. Serjeant, "Spencer's Regiment," Continental Army, February 1st, 1777; Ensign, ditto, May 12th, 1779; Lieutenant and Quartermaster ditto, July 10th, 1779; discharged at the close of the war.

Ogden Nathaniel. Quartermaster, Continental Army.

Periam, Joseph. Quartermaster, First Battalion, Second

Establishment, November 28th, 1776; retired September 26th, 1780.

Smith, Israel. Captain and Quartermaster, General Heard's Brigade, Continental Army, March 1st, 1779; also Assistant Quartermaster, Quartermaster's Department.

PAYMASTERS.

* Shute, William. (Original member.) Captain and Paymaster, Second Battalion, First Establishment, November 28th, 1775; Captain and Paymaster, Second Battalion, Second Establishment, November 28th, 1776; resigned April 2d, 1778; appointed Ensign and Paymaster, Second Regiment, to date June 17th, 1780; discharged at the close of the war; Captain by brevet.

Spencer, Robert. Paymaster, " Spencer's Regiment," Continental Army.

SURGEONS.

Barnet, William M. Surgeon, First Battalion, First Establishment, December 8th, 1775; Surgeon, First Battalion, Second Establishment, November 28th, 1776; Surgeon, First Regiment; resigned.

Bloomfield, Moses. Surgeon, United States Hospital, Continental Army, May 14th, 1777.

Burnet, William. (Original member.) Chief Physician and Surgeon, General Hospital, Continental Army; also Surgeon, militia.

Burnet, William, Jr. Surgeon, General Hospital, Continental Army.

Campbell, George [W]. (Original member.) Surgeon, Hospital of Flying Camp, Continental Army, April 11th, 1777.

* Campfield, Jazeb. (Original member.) Surgeon, " Spencer's Regiment." Continental Army, January 1st, 1777; Senior Physician, Continental Army; discharged at the close of the war.

Cochran, John. Surgeon General in General Hospital, April 11th, 1777; Chief Physician and Surgeon to the Army, October 19th, 1780.

Dunham, Lewis F. (Original member.) Surgeon, Third Battalion, First Establishment, February 21st, 1776; Surgeon, Third Battalion, Second Establishment, November 28th, 1776; Surgeon, Third Regiment, resigned.

* Elmer, Ebenezer. (Original member.) Ensign, Captain Bloomfield's company, Third Battalion, First Establishment, February 9th, 1776; Second Lieutenant, ditto, April 9th, 1776; Surgeon's Mate, Third Battalion, Second Establishment, November 28th, 1776; transferred to Second Battalion, ditto; Surgeon, Second Battalion, Second Establishment, July 5th, 1778; Surgeon, Second Regiment, September 26th, 1780; discharged at the close of the war.

Ervin, David. Surgeon, First Regiment, September 26th, 1780; also Surgeon's Mate, militia.

* Harris, Jacob. (Original member.) Surgeon's Mate, First Battalion, Second Establishment, November 28th, 1776; Surgeon's Mate, Fourth Battalion, Second Establishment, February 26th, 1777; Surgeon's Mate, First Regiment, September 26th, 1780; Surgeon, Third Regiment, November 16th, 1782; discharged at the close of the war.

McCarter, Charles. Surgeon, "Morgan's Rifle Corps," Continental Army, June 10th, 1777.

Otto, Frederick. Surgeon in General Hospital, May 1st, 1777.

Reed, Thomas. Surgeon, "Livingston's Regiment," Continental Army, December 18th, 1776.

Riker, John B. Surgeon, Fourth Battalion, Second Establishment, November 28th, 1776; retired September 26th, 1780.

Scott, Moses. Surgeon in General Hospital, Continental Army; also Surgeon, militia.

Tunison, Garret. Surgeon, "Lamb's Artillery," (Second Regiment Artillery), Continental Army; discharged at the close of the war.

Vickars, Samuel. Surgeon's Mate in General Hospital, Continental Army; Surgeon, ditto, April 14th, 1777.

Wilson, Lewis. Surgeon's Mate in General Hospital, Continental Army, January, 1778; Surgeon, ditto, June 30th, 1779.

Witherspoon, John. Surgeon in General Hospital, Continental Army.

SURGEONS' MATES.

*Appleton, Abraham. (Original member.) Surgeon's Mate, Second Battalion, First Establishment, December 21st, 1775; discharged with battalion. (See, also, Lieutenants.)

Ball, Stephen. Surgeon's Mate, First Regiment, September 26th, 1780; resigned.

Dorsey, John. Surgeon's Mate, "Spencer's Regiment," Continental Army, January 1st, 1777.

*‡ Elmer, Moses G. (Original member.) Surgeon's Mate, Second Battalion, Second Establishment, August 28th, 1778; Surgeon's Mate, Second Regiment, September 26th, 1780; discharged at the close of the war.

Henry, Robert R. Surgeon's Mate in General Hospital, Continental Army, March 17th, 1777.

Loree (or Loring), Ephraim. Surgeon's Mate, Third Battalion, Second Establishment, November 28th, 1776; Surgeon's Mate, Third Regiment, September 26th, 1780; resigned.

Morris, Jonathan F. Surgeon's Mate in General Hospital, Continental Army, March 6th, 1780; also Lieutenant, "Proctor's Regiment of Artillery," Continental Army; also Surgeon, militia.

Read, Thomas C. Surgeon's Mate, Third Battalion, First Establishment, February 9th, 1776; discharged with battalion.

Stockton, Ebenezer. (Original member.) Surgeon's Mate in General Hospital, Continental Army, September 20th, 1777.

CHAPLAINS.

Armstrong, James F. (Original member.) Chaplain, Second Maryland Brigade, Continental Army, July 17th, 1778; also private, militia.

Cox, ——. Chaplain, First Battalion, Second Establishment, November 28th, 1776; retired September 26th, 1780.

Hunter, Andrew. (Original member.) Chaplain, Third Battalion, Second Establishment, June 1st, 1777; Chaplain to General Maxwell's Brigade, June 15th, 1777; Chaplain, Third Regiment and Brigade, September 26th, 1780; taken prisoner; discharged at the close of the war; also Chaplain, militia.

Mason, John. Chaplain, Continental Army; discharged at the close of the war; also Chaplain, militia.

McWhorter, Alexander. Chaplain of Division, Continental Army.

Spencer, Elihu. Chaplain in Hospital, Middle District, Continental Army, October 20th, 1777.

COMMISSARY-GENERAL OF PRISONERS.

Beatty, John. (Original member.) Commissary-General of Prisoners, May 28th, 1778; resigned March 31st, 1780; Captain, Fifth Pennsylvania Battalion, Continental Line, October 12th, 1776; taken prisoner at Fort Washington, November 16th, 1776.

COMMISSARY-GENERAL OF ISSUES.

Stewart, Charles. Colonel, Battalion Minute Men, New Jersey Militia, February 15th, 1776; Commissary-General, New Jersey Militia; Commissary-General of Issues, Continental Army, June 18th, 1777, to July, 1782.

CAPTAINS.

Anderson, John. First Lieutenant, Captain Reading's company, Third Battalion, First Establishment, February 7th, 1776; resigned; Captain, Fourth Battalion, Second Establishment, November 28th, 1776; retired September 26th, 1780; also Captain, militia.

Anderson, Joseph I. Ensign, Captain Sharp's company, Third Battalion, First Establishment; Second Lieutenant, ditto, July 19th, 1776; First Lieutenant, Captain Mott's company, Third Battalion, Second Establishment, November 29th, 1776; Captain, ditto, October 26th, 1777; Captain, Third Regiment; Captain and Paymaster, Third Regiment, to date April 1st, 1779; Captain, First Regiment; discharged at the close of the war.

‡ Baldwin, Daniel. (Original member.) First Lieutenant, Captain Morris' company, First Battalion, First Establishment, November 8th, 1775; Captain, First Battalion, Second Establishment, November 29th, 1776; severely wounded—lost a leg at the battle of Germantown, October 4th, 1777; discharged March 1st, 1779.

* Ballard, Jeremiah. (Original member.) Second Lieutenant, Captain Reading's company, Third Battalion, First Establishment, February 17th, 1776; First Lieutenant, Captain Doughty's company, Third Battalion, Second Establishment, November 29th, 1776; Captain, ditto, October 26th, 1777; Captain, Third Regiment, September 23d, 1780; Captain, Second Regiment; discharged at the close of the war.

* Barton, William. (Original member.) Ensign, Fourth Battalion, Second Establishment, November 28th, 1776; Second Lieutenant, Captain Lyon's company, ditto, February 17th, 1777; First Lieutenant, ditto; Lieutenant, First Regiment, to date November 1st, 1777; Quartermaster, ditto, to date March 11th, 1780; Captain, ditto, December 27th, 1781; discharged at the close of the war.

Bond, William. Captain, Fourth Battalion, Second Establishment, November 28th, 1776; retired September 26th, 1780; also Lieutenant Colonel, militia.

Bonnel, James. (Original member.) Lieutenant, " Spencer's Regiment," Continental Army, February 1st, 1777; Adjutant, ditto, September 1st, 1778; Captain, ditto, April 24th, 1779; discharged at the close of the war; also Captain, militia.

Brearley, Joseph. Captain, Second Battalion, First Establishment, November 20th, 1775; Captain, Second Battalion, Second Establishment, November 29th, 1776; retired February 5th, 1777; also Major, militia.

Broderick, James. Captain, "Spencer's Regiment," Continental Army, February 18th, 1777; resigned; also Major, militia; Captain, First Regiment, Sussex; Captain, Third Battalion, ditto; First Major, Second Regiment, Sussex, February 28th, 1777; resigned; also Captain, Continental Army.

Bull, William. Captain, "Spencer's Regiment," Continental Army.

Clark, Thomas. First Lieutenant, Eastern Company of Artillery, State Troops, March 1st, 1776; Captain-Lieutenant, ditto; Captain, ditto, January 8th, 1778. Officers in this artillery served in General Knox's brigade of artillery during the war.

Colfax, William. Lieutenant in "Commander-in-Chief's Guard," Continental Army; Captain, ditto.

Craig, John. Captain, "Fourth Regiment, Light Dragoons," Continental Army.

Crane, William. Lieutenant, "Spencer's Regiment," Continental Army; Captain, ditto, March, 1777.

* Dayton, Jonathan. (Original member.) Paymaster, Third Battalion, First Establishment, February 7th, 1776; Paymaster, Third Battalion, Second Establishment; Lieutenant and Paymaster, Third Regiment, to date February 1st, 1779; Major and Aid-de-Camp to Major-General Sullivan, May 1st, 1779; Captain, Third Regiment, to date March 30th, 1780; prisoner of war, November 4th, 1780; Captain, First Regiment; discharged at the close of the war.

* D'Hart, Cyrus. (Original member.) Ensign, Captain Daniel Piatt's company, First Battalion, First Establishment, September 18th, 1776; Lieutenant and Paymaster, First Regiment; Captain-Lieutenant, ditto, to date March 11th, 1780; Captain, ditto, January 1st, 1781; Captain, Second Regiment; discharged at the close of the war.

Dickerson, Peter. Captain, Third Battalion, First Establishment, February 7th, 1776; Captain, Third Battalion, Second Establishment, November 29th, 1776; retired September 26th, 1780.

Dillon, James. First Lieutenant, Captain Faulkner's company, Second Battalion, First Establishment, November 13th, 1775; Captain, Second Battalion, First Establishment, May 10th, 1776; Captain, Second Battalion, Second Establishment, November 29th, 1776; retired September 26th, 1780.

Edgar, David. First Lieutenant, Fourth Battalion, Second Establishment, November 28th, 1776; First Lieutenant, Captain Lyon's company, ditto, February 17th, 1777; Captain, ditto; resigned; Lieutenant, " Sheldon's Regiment, Light Dragoons," Continental Army; Captain, ditto, November 27th, 1778; discharged at the close of the war; also First Lieutenant, militia.

Elmer, Eli. (Original member.) Second Lieutenant and Captain, Western Company of Artillery, New Jersey State Troops; First Lieutenant, ditto, February 1st, 1777. (Officers of this artillery served in General Knox's brigade of artillery during the war.)

Flahaven, John. Second Lieutenant, Captain Daniel Piatt's company, First Battalion, First Establishment, December 16th, 1775; Second Lieutenant, Captain Conway's company, First Battalion, Second Establishment, November 29th, 1776; prisoner of war, April 22d, 1777; Captain, First Regiment, September 26th, 1780; resigned.

Flanningham (or Flanagan), Samuel. First Lieutenant, Captain Sharp's company, Third Battalion, First Establishment, February 9th, 1776; First Lieutenant, Captain Dickerson's company, Third Battalion, Second Establishment, November 29th, 1776; Captain, ditto, retired; also Major, militia.

Foreman, Thomas M. Captain, Continental Army.

Gifford, William. Second Lieutenant, Captain Bloomfield's company, Third Battalion, First Establishment, February 7th, 1776; First Lieutenant, ditto; Captain, Third Battalion, Second Establishment, November 29th, 1776; Captain, Third Regiment; prisoner of war, January 30th, 1780; resigned.

* Heard, James. (Original member.) Cornet, " Lee's Legion," Continental Army, April 1st, 1779; Lieutenant and Pay-

master, ditto, February 1st, 1780; Captain, ditto; discharged at the close of the war.

* Heard, John. (Original member.) Lieutenant, "Moylan's Regiment," Continental Army, January 20th, 1777; Captain, ditto, February 8th, 1778; also Second Lieutenant, militia. (Eastern Company of Artillery.)

* Helms, William. (Original member.) Ensign, Second Battalion, First Establishment, November 7th, 1775; Lieutenant, Captain Shaw's company, ditto, December 25th, 1775; Second Lieutenant, Captain Brearley's company, Second Battalion, Second Establishment, November 29th, 1776; First Lieutenant, Captain Luce's company, ditto, February 5th, 1777; Captain, ditto, December 1st, 1777; Captain, Second Regiment, September 26th, 1780; Major by brevet; discharged at the close of the war; also Captain, militia.

* Hendry, Samuel. (Original member.) Ensign, Captain Lawrie's company, Second Battalion, First Establishment, November 27th, 1775; Second Lieutenant, ditto, September 5th, 1776; Second Lieutenant, Captain Stout's company, Second Battalion, Second Establishment, November 29th, 1776; First Lieutenant, Captain Anderson's company, ditto, February 5th, 1777; Captain-Lieutenant, Second Regiment; Captain, ditto, to date July 5th, 1779; discharged at the close of the war.

Hennion, Cornelius. Ensign, Captain Potter's company, Third Battalion, First Establishment, February 7th, 1776; Secone Lieutenant, ditto, July 19th, 1776; First Lieutenant, Captain Gifford's company, Third Battalion, Second Establishment, November 29th, 1776; Captain, ditto; severely wounded at Short Hills, New Jersey, June 26th, 1777, and discharged on account of wounds, April 1st, 1778.

Herron, James. Captain, "Congress' Own Regiment," Continental Army.

Holmes, James. Captain, Fourth Battalion, Second Establishment, November 28th, 1776; retired September 26th, 1780; also Captain, militia.

* Holmes, John. (Original member.) Second Lieutenant, Captain Longstreet's company, First Battalion, First Establishment, December 16th, 1775; Second Lieutenant, Captain Polhemus' company, First Battalion, Second Establishment, November 29th, 1776; Captain, First Regiment, to date February 1st, 1779; discharged at the close of the war.

* Holmes, Jonathan. (Original member.) Second Lieutenant, Fourth Battalion, Second Establishment, November 28th, 1776; Second Lieutenant, Captain Forman's company, ditto, February 17th, 1777; First Lieutenant, ditto; Lieutenant, Second Regiment; Captain, ditto, to date April 16th, 1780; prisoner of war; discharged at the close of the war; also Second Lieutenant, militia.

* Howell, John. (Original member.) Ensign, Captain Howell's company, First Battalion, Second Establishment, November 29th, 1776; Lieutenant, First Regiment, to date October 29th, 1777; Captain, ditto, November 20th, 1781; discharged at the close of the war.

Howell, Silas. Captain, First Battalion, First Establishment, November 14th, 1775; Captain, First Battalion, Second Establishment, November 29th, 1776; retired September 26th, 1780.

Imlay, William Eugene. Captain, Third Battalion, First Establishment, February 7th, 1776; discharged with battalion; also Captain, militia.

Kinsey, Jonathan. Captain, Fourth Battalion, Second Establishment, November 28th, 1776; retired September 26th, 1780; also Captain, militia.

Kirkpatrick, David. Lieutenant, "Spencer's Regiment," Continental Army; Captain, ditto.

* Lane, Derrick. (Original member.) Second Lieutenant, Fourth Battalion, Second Establishment, November 28th, 1776; Second Lieutenant, Captain Hollinshead's company, Second Battalion, Second Establishment, February 5th, 1777; Lieutenant and Quartermaster, Second Regiment, to date April 3d, 1779; Captain-Lieutenant, ditto, to date July 5th, 1778; Captain, ditto, February 11th, 1783; discharged at close of the war; also Second Lieutenant, militia.

* Leonard, Nathaniel. (Original member. Dropped from

Rolls 1799.) Ensign, Captain Sharp's company, Third Battalion, First Establishment, February 9th, 1776; Second Lieutenant, Captain Gordon's company, Third Battalion, Second Establishment, November 29th, 1776; First Lieutenant, ditto, October 1st, 1777; Lieutenant, Third Regiment; Captain-Lieutenant, First Regiment, March 30th, 1780; Captain, Third Regiment, September 6th, 1781; discharged at the close of the war; also Captain, militia.

Lloyd, Bateman. First Lieutenant, Captain Kinsey's company, Fourth Battalion, Second Establishment, February 17, 1777; Captain, ditto, November 12th, 1777; Captain, Third Regiment, September 26th, 1780; Captain, Second Regiment; taken prisoner, February 27th, 1778; exchanged April 1st, 1781; resigned; also Captain, militia.

§ Lloyd, Richard. (Original member.) First Lieutenant, Captain Imlay's company, Third Battalion, First Establishment, February 7th, 1776; Captain, "Hazen's Regiment" (Second Canadian), Continental Army, September 20th, 1777; discharged at the close of the war; Major by brevet.

Longstreet, Elias. Captain, First Battalion, First Establishment, December 16th, 1775; Captain, First Battalion, Second Establishment, November 29th, 1776; prisoner of war; retired September 26th, 1780.

Luce, Henry. First Lieutenant, Captain Shaw's company, Second Battalion, First Establishment, December 25th, 1775; First Lieutenant, Captain Stout's company, Second Battalion, Second Establishment, November 29th, 1776; Captain, Second Battalion, ditto, February 5th, 1777; resigned April, 1779; also Captain, militia.

* Martin, Absalom. (Original member.) Paymaster, Fourth Battalion, Second Establishment, November 28th, 1776; Lieutenant, First Regiment, to date February 1st, 1779; Lieutenant and Paymaster, ditto, to date November 1st, 1779; Captain, First Regiment, January 6th, 1783; discharged at the close of the war.

Martin, Jacob. Captain, Fourth Battalion, Second Establishment.

Maxwell, Anthony. Lieutenant, " Spencer's Regiment,"
Continental Army ; Captain, ditto.

Maxwell, James. First Lieutenant, Captain Scott's company, Second Battalion, First Establishment, December 9th,
1775 ; First Lieutenant, Captain Shute's company, Second Battalion, Second Establishment, November 29th, 1776; First
Lieutenant, Captain Reading's company, ditto, February 5th,
1777; Captain, ditto; retired September 26th, 1780.

Mead, Yellis (or Giles). (Original member.) First Lieutenant, Captain Meeker's company, First Battalion, First Establishment, December 10th, 1775; First Lieutenant, Captain
Conway's company, First Battalion, Second Establishment,
November 29th, 1776; Captain, ditto, October 29th, 1777; Captain, First Regiment, September 26th, 1780; discharged at the
close of the war.

Meeker, Joseph. Captain, First Battalion, First Establishment, December 9th, 1775; discharged with battalion.

Mercer, John. Ensign, Captain Howell's company, First
Battalion, First Establishment; First Lieutenant, ditto, November 14th, 1775; First Lieutenant, Captain Morris' company, First Battalion, Second Establishment, November 29th,
1776; Captain, ditto, February 15th, 1777; prisoner of war; exchanged November 6th, 1780; retired September 26th, 1780.

* ‡ Mitchell, Alexander. (Original member. Dropped from
Rolls September, 1783.) First Lieutenant, Fourth Battalion,
Second Establishment, November 28th, 1776; First Lieutenant,
Captain Holmes' company, ditto, February 17th, 1777; Cap-
tain, ditto, November 1st, 1777; Captain, First Regiment, Sep-
tember 26th, 1780; discharged at the close of the war; also
First Lieutenant, militia.

Morrison, Isaac. First Lieutenant, Captain M'Mires'
company, First Battalion, First Establishment, December 15th,
1775; First Lieutenant, Captain Polhemus' company, First Battalion, Second Establishment, November 29th, 1776; Captain,
ditto; retired September 26th, 1780.

Mott, John. First Lieutenant, Captain Patterson's company, Third Battalion, First Establishment, February 9th,

1776; Captain, Third Battalion, Second Establishment, November 29th, 1776; retired, September 26th, 1780; also Captain, militia.

Neeley, Abraham. Captain, "Spencer's Regiment," Continental Army.

Parkhurst, John. Captain, Continental Army.

Patterson, Thomas. Captain, Third Battalion, First Establishment, February 9th, 1776; Captain, Third Battalion, Second Establishment, November 29th, 1776; retired September 26th, 1780.

Pemberton, Robert. (Original member.) Lieutenant, "Spencer's Regiment," Continental Army, June 14th, 1777; Adjutant, ditto, October 10th, 1777; Captain, ditto, January 1st, 1778; discharged at the close of the war.

* Phillips, Jonathan. (Original member.) Second Lieutenant, Captain Brearley's company, Second Battalion, First Establishment, November 20th, 1775; First Lieutenant, Captain Shaw's company, Second Battalion, Second Establishment, November 29th, 1776; First Lieutenant, Captain Yard's company, ditto, February 5th, 1777; Captain, ditto, December 1st, 1777; Captain, Second Regiment, September 26th, 1780; discharged at the close of the war; also Captain, militia.

Piatt, Jacob. (Original member.) Ensign, Captain M'Mires' company, First Battalion, First Establishment, December 15th, 1775; Second Lieutenant, Captain Longstreet's company, First Battalion, Second Establishment, November 29th, 1776; Adjutant, First Battalion, ditto; Lieutenant and Adjutant, First Regiment; Captain-Lieutenant, ditto, to date February 2d, 1779; Captain by brevet; Captain, ditto; resigned, to date March 11th, 1780.

* Piatt, William. (Original member.) Private, First Battalion, Second Establishment; Serjeant, ditto; Lieutenant, First Regiment; Captain, ditto, to date March 11th, 1780; discharged at the close of the war.

Pike, Zebulon. Cornet, "Moylan's Regiment," Continental Army, March 1st, 1777; Adjutant, ditto, November 1st,

1777; Lieutenant, ditto, March 15th, 1778; Paymaster, ditto; Captain, ditto, December 25th, 1778.

Potter, Samuel. Captain, Third Battalion, First Establishment, February 9th, 1776; discharged with battalion.

Reading, Thomas. Captain, Third Battalion, First Establishment, February 9th, 1776; discharged with battalion.

Sandford, John. Captain, "Spencer's Regiment," Continental Army.

Sharp, Anthony. Captain, Third Battalion, First Establishment, February 9th, 1776; discharged with battalion; also, Major, militia.

Shaw, Archibald. Captain, Second Battalion, First Establishment, December 25th, 1775; Captain, Second Battalion, Second Establishment, November 29th, 1776; retired, February 5th, 1777.

Sparks, John. Ensign, Captain Faulkner's company, Second Battalion, First Establishment, November 13th, 1775; Second Lieutenant, Captain Dillon's company, ditto, May 10th, 1776; Second Lieutenant, Captain Lawrie's company, Second Battalion, Second Establishment, November 29th, 1776; First Lieutenant, Captain Cumming's company, ditto, February 5th, 1777; Captain, ditto; retired September 26th, 1780.

Van Anglen, John. Ensign, Captain Polhemus' company, First Battalion, First Establishment; First Lieutenant, ditto, November 22d, 1775; First Lieutenant, Captain Howell's company, First Battalion, Second Establishment, November 29th, 1776; Captain, ditto; retired September 26th, 1780.

Wade, Noadiah. Captain, Fourth Battalion, Second Establishment, February 17th, 1777; retired September 26th, 1780.

Weatherby, Benjamin. Captain, "Spencer's Regiment," Continental Army, February 23d, 1777; discharged at the close of the war.

Westcott, John. First Lieutenant, Western Artillery, Western Company, Artillery, State Troops, March 1st, 1776; Captain-Lieutenant, ditto; Captain, ditto. Officers of this artillery served in General Knox's brigade of artillery during the war.

* Weyman, Abel. (Original member.) Ensign, Fourth Battalion, Second Establishment, November 28th, 1776; Second Lieutenant, Captain Anderson's company, ditto, February 17th, 1777; First Lieutenant, ditto, November 1st, 1777; Lieutenant, Second Regiment, September 26th, 1780; Captain-Lieutenant, ditto, April 16th, 1780; Captain, ditto, January 1st, 1781; discharged at the close of the war; also Ensign, militia.

Whittall, Benjamin. Second Lieutenant, Western Company Artillery, State Troops; First Lieutenant, ditto; Captain-Lieutenant, ditto. (This artillery assigned to General Knox's brigade of artillery.) Captain, Colonel Newcomb's battalion, State Troops.

Wool, Isaiah. Captain, Artillery, Continental Army.

Yard, Thomas. First Lieutenant, Captain Brearley's company, Second Battalion, First Establishment, November 20th, 1775; Captain, Second Battalion, Second Establishment, November 29th, 1776; retired September 26th, 1780.

LIEUTENANTS.

Anderson, Augustine. Lieutenant, Continental Army.

† § Anderson, James. (Original member.) Lieutenant, " Hazen's Regiment," (Second Canadian), Continental Army; discharged at the close of the war.

Appleton, Abraham. (Original member.) Second Lieutenant, Captain Yard's company, Second Battalion, Second Establishment, February 5th, 1777; Ensign, Second Regiment; Lieutenant, ditto, to date December 1st, 1777; discharged at the close of the war; Captain by brevet. (See, also, Surgeons' Mates.)

* Blair, John. (Original member.) Ensign, Fourth Battalion, Second Establishment, November 28th, 1776; Ensign, Captain Kinsey's company, ditto, February 17th, 1777; Second Lieutenant, ditto; First Lieutenant, Captain Holmes' com-

pany, ditto; Lieutenant, Third Regiment, to date December 2d, 1777; Lieutenant, First Regiment; discharged at the close of the war; Captain by brevet; also Ensign, militia.

* Bonham, Absalom. (Original member.) Second Lieutenant, Fourth Battalion, Second Establishment, November 1st, 1777; transferred to First Battalion; First Lieutenant, ditto, March 27th, 1780; Ensign, First Regiment; Lieutenant, ditto, to date March 27th, 1780; discharged at the close of the war; Captain by brevet.

Brown, John. Private, "Forman's Regiment," Continental Army; Serjeant, "Spencer's Regiment," Continental Army, July 1st, 1777; Lieutenant, Captain Edgar's troop, "Sheldon's Regiment, Light Dragoons," Continental Army.

* Buck, Joseph. (Original member.) Serjeant, Second Battalion, Second Establishment; Ensign, Second Regiment, to date February 1st, 1779; Lieutenant, ditto, January 1st, 1781; discharged at the close of the war; Captain by brevet.

* Burrowes, Eden. (Original member.) Serjeant, First Battalion, Second Establishment; Lieutenant, First Regiment, to date January 4th, 1778; discharged at the close of the war; Captain by brevet.

Colyer, Thomas. Lieutenant, Continental Army.

* Conn, Samuel. (Original member.) Second Lieutenant, Captain Kinsey's company, Fourth Battalion, Second Establishment, February 17th, 1777; Lieutenant, Second Regiment, to date November 12th, 1777; discharged at the close of the war; Captain by brevet; also Lieutenant, militia.

† Giles, James. (Original member.) Adjutant, Artillery, Continental Army; Lieutenant, ditto.

Gildersleeve, Finch. Lieutenant, "Spencer's Regiment," Continental Army.

* Kersey, William. (Original member.) Private, Third Battalion, First Establishment; Private, Captain Ross' company, Third Battalion, Second Establishment; Second Lieutenant, ditto, November 1st, 1777; Ensign, Third Regiment; Lieutenant, ditto, to date March 30th, 1780; Lieutenant, First Regiment; discharged at the close of the war; Captain by brevet.

Kollock, Shepherd. (Original member.) Lieutenant, Artillery, Continental Army; Captain by brevet.

Lane, Aaron. Ensign, Captain Stout's company, Second Battalion, First Establishment, December 18th, 1775; Second Lieutenant, Captain Yard's company, Second Battalion, Second Establishment, November 29th, 1776; Second Lieutenant, Captain Anderson's company, ditto, February 5th, 1777; Lieutenant, Second Regiment; resigned to date February 3d, 1779.

Little, Eleazer. Lieutenant, "Baldwin's Regiment of Artificers," Continental Army, March 2d, 1777.

McCollum, John. Lieutenant, Continental Army.

Meeker, Uzal. Ensign, "Spencer's Regiment," Continental Army, February 10th, 1777; Lieutenant, ditto, February, 10th, 1779; discharged at the close of the war.

Munn, John. Lieutenant, Continental Army; prisoner of war, September, 1780.

Nash, ——. Lieutenant, "Patton's Regiment," Continental Army.

Neglee, Samuel. Ensign, Captain Howell's company, Second Battalion, First Establishment, November 29th, 1775; Second Lieutenant, Captain Dillon's company, Second Battalion, Second Establishment, November 29th, 1776; Lieutenant, Second Regiment; resigned April 8th, 1780.

Ogden, Barne. Ensign, "Spencer's Regiment," Continental Army, February 8th, 1777; Lieutenant, ditto, September 16th, 1777.

Oliver, William. Lieutenant, Continental Army.

Orr, John. Lieutenant, "Spencer's Regiment," Continental Army, October 10th, 1778; discharged at the close of the war.

* Osmun, Benajah. (Original member.) Second Lieutenant and Quartermaster, Second Battalion, Second Establishment, January 1st, 1777; resigned; Ensign, Second Regiment, to date September 12th, 1778; prisoner of war, April 25th, 1780; Lieutenant, ditto, January 1st, 1781; discharged at the close of the war; Captain by brevet.

Parkinson, Henry. Lieutenant, Continental Army.

Parrit, Silas. Second Lieutenant, First Battalion, Second Establishment, January 4th, 1778; Ensign, First Regiment; Lieutenant, ditto, November 27th, 1780; discharged at the close of the war.

Patterson, ——. Lieutenant, " Forman's Regiment," Continental Army.

Paul, James. Private, Second Battalion, Second Establishment; Ensign, ditto, July 1st, 1777; prisoner of war, April 3d, 1779; Ensign, Second Regiment; Lieutenant, ditto, to date April 16th, 1780; discharged at the close of the war.

* Peck, John. (Original member.) Paymaster, Second Battalion, Second Establishment, April 2d, 1778; Paymaster, Second Regiment; resigned as Paymaster, and commissioned Lieutenant, ditto, January 1st, 1781; discharged at the close of the war; Captain by brevet; also Captain, militia.

Reckless, Anthony. (Original member.) Lieutenant, " Regiment Sappers and Miners," Continental Army; discharged at the close of the war.

Reed, John. Ensign, First Battalion, Second Establishment; Lieutenant, Third Regiment, to date February 1st, 1779; Lieutenant, First Regiment; discharged at the close of the war; Captain by brevet.

* Rhea, Jonathan. (Original member.) Ensign, Captain Anderson's company, Second Battalion, Second Establishment, January 1st, 1777; Second Lieutenant, ditto, April 1st, 1778; Ensign, Second Regiment; Lieutenant, ditto, January 1st, 1781; Captain by brevet.

* Ruecastle, John. (Original member.) Private, Third Battalion, First Establishment; Private, Captain Patterson's company, Third Battalion, Second Establishment; Second Lieutenant, Third Battalion, Second Establishment, November 1st, 1777; Ensign, Third Regiment; Lieutenant, ditto, to date April 7th, 1779; Lieutenant, First Regiment; discharged at the close of the war; Captain by brevet.

Rutan, Peter. Lieutenant, " Livingston's Regiment," Continental Army.

* Seeley, Samuel. (Original member.) Second Lieuten-

ant, First Battalion, Second Establishment, October 4th, 1777; First Lieutenant, ditto, March 11th, 1780; Ensign, First Regiment; Lieutenant, ditto, to date March 11th, 1780; discharged at the close of the war; Captain by brevet.

Shreve, John. Ensign, Captain Brearley's company, Second Battalion, First Establishment, July 25th, 1776; Ensign, Captain Lawrie's company, Second Battalion, Second Establishment, November 29th, 1776; Ensign, Captain Hollinshead's company, ditto, February 5th, 1777; Second Lieutenant, ditto, November 1st, 1777; Ensign, Second Regiment; Lieutenant, ditto, to date February 3d, 1779; resigned.

* Shute, Samuel. (Original member.) Ensign, Captain Dillon's company, Second Battalion, First Establishment, August 26th, 1776; Ensign, Captain Shute's company, Second Battalion, Second Establishment, November 29th, 1776; Ensign, Captain Cumming's company, ditto, February 5th, 1777; Second Lieutenant, ditto, January 1st, 1778; Ensign, Second Regiment; Lieutenant, ditto, to date April 8th, 1780; discharged at the close of the war; Captain by brevet.

Sitcher, William. Lieutenant, "Spencer's Regiment," Continental Army.

Smith, Hiram. Private, Continental Army; Serjeant, ditto; Lieutenant, ditto.

† Snowden, Jonathan. (Original member.) Second Lieutenant, First Battalion, Second Establishment, April 26th, 1777; First Lieutenant, ditto, October 26th, 1779; Ensign, First Regiment; Lieutenant, ditto; Aid-de-Camp to Brigadier General Edward Hand, of Pennsylvania; Lieutenant, commanding company, "Lee's Legion," Continental Army; discharged at the close of the war.

* Stout, Abraham. (Original member.) Serjeant, Third Battalion, First Establishment, February 7th, 1776; Ensign, ditto, October 29th, 1776; Second Lieutenant, Captain Stout's company, Second Battalion, Second Establishment, November 29th, 1776; Ensign, Second Regiment; Lieutenant, ditto, to date December 1st, 1777; prisoner of war, April 5th, 1778; ex-

changed December 3d, 1780; discharged at the close of the war; Captain by brevet.

* Stout, Wessel T. (Original member.) Second Lieutenant, Fourth Battalion, Second Establishment, November 1st, 1777; transferred to Third Battalion; Ensign, Third Regiment; Lieutenant, ditto, May 12th, 1782; Lieutenant, First Regiment; discharged at the close of the war; Captain by brevet.

Taulman, Peter. Lieutenant, " Spencer's Regiment," Continental Army.

Van Cleaf, William. Serjeant, " Service in Canada," 1775; Lieutenant, September, 1777; also Captain, militia.

Van Dyke, John. Second Lieutenant, Eastern Company Artillery, State Troops, March 1st, 1776; First Lieutenant, ditto, December 4th, 1776; Captain-Lieutenant, ditto. Officers of this artillery served in General Knox's brigade of artillery during the war.

* Walker, George. (Original member.) Served as Captain in Second Battalion, Second Establishment, as a volunteer without pay; Ensign, Second Regiment, September 26th, 1780; Lieutenant, ditto, January 1st, 1781; discharged at the close of the war; Captain by brevet.

Wilkison, Nathan. Serjeant, Captain Dickerson's company, Third Battalion, First Establishment; Serjeant, ditto, Third Battalion, Second Establishment; Second Lieutenant and Quartermaster, ditto, November 1st, 1777; Ensign, Third Regiment; Lieutenant, ditto, to date March 7th, 1780; Lieutenant, First Regiment; resigned.

FIRST LIEUTENANTS.

Bostwick, William. First Lieutenant, Captain Gordon's company, Third Battalion, Second Establishment, November 29th, 1776; retired September 26th, 1780.

Bowen, Seth. (Original member.) Second Lieutenant, Captain Howell's company, Second Battalion, First Establishment, November 29th, 1775; First Lieutenant, Captain Yard's company, Second Battalion, Second Establishment, November 29th, 1776; First Lieutenant, Captain Lawrie's company, ditto, February 5th, 1777; declined; also Captain-Lieutenant, militia (Western Company of Artillery).

Carnes, Zophar. First Lieutenant, Fourth Battalion, Second Establishment, November 28th, 1776; First Lieutenant, Captain Wade's company, ditto, February 17th, 1777; retired September 26th, 1780; also Captain, militia.

Clark, William. Ensign, Captain Ross' company, Third Battalion, First Establishment; Second Lieutenant, ditto, October 29th, 1776; Second Lieutenant, Captain Ross' company, Third Battalion, Second Establishment, November 29th, 1776; First Lieutenant, ditto, January 1st, 1777; wounded at the battle of Germantown, October 4th, 1777; discharged—wounds.

Costigin, Lewis J. First Lieutenant, Captain Conway's company, First Battalion, First Establishment, November 21st, 1775; retired September 17th, 1776; First Lieutenant, Captain Baldwin's company, First Battalion, Second Establishment, November 30th, 1776; prisoner of war, November 13th, 1776; exchanged December 18th, 1778; retired September 26th, 1780.

Curtis, Marmaduke. First Lieutenant, Captain Rosecrantz's company, Third Battalion, Second Establishment, November 29th, 1776; retired September 26th, 1780; also Captain, militia.

Duclos, Francis. Ensign, Captain Scott's company, Second Battalion, First Establishment, December 9th, 1775; taken prisoner at Three Rivers, June 8th, 1776; Second Lieutenant, Third Battalion, First Establishment; First Lieutenant, Second Battalion, Second Establishment; retired September 26th, 1780.

Dunham, Stephen. First Lieutenant, Captain Dickerson's company, Third Battalion, First Establishment, February 7th, 1776; resigned; Ensign, Captain Baldwin's company, First Battalion, Second Establishment, November 29th, 1776; retired September 26th, 1780.

Edsall, Richard.   First Lieutenant, Captain Forman's company, Fourth Battalion, Second Establishment, February 17th, 1777; retired September 26th, 1780; also Captain, militia.

Fisher, Hendrick.   First Lieutenant, Captain Daniel Piatt's company, First Battalion, First Establishment, December 16th, 1775; First Lieutenant, Captain Piatt's company, First Battalion, Second Establishment, November 29th, 1776; retired September 16th, 1780.

Ford, Mahlon.   (Original member.)   Second Lieutenant, Third Battalion, Second Establishment, November 28th, 1777; First Lieutenant, ditto; retired September 26th, 1780; Captain by brevet.

Fries, Henry.   First Lieutenant, Captain Shute's company, Second Battalion, First Establishment, November 28th, 1775; missing in action at Three Rivers, June 8th, 1776.

Harker, ——.   First Lieutenant, Captain Lyon's company, Fourth Battalion, Second Establishment; resigned September 26th, 1780.

Harrison, Isaac.   First Lieutenant, Captain Gifford's company, Third Battalion, Second Establishment.

Kemper, Jacob.   Ensign, Captain Howell's company, First Battalion, First Establishment, April 1st, 1776; discharged with battalion; First Lieutenant, Captain Winslow's company, "Stevens' Regiment of Artillery," Continental Army, November 9th, 1776.

Little, Theodore.   First Lieutenant, Continental Army.

Martin, John.   First Lieutenant, Fourth Battalion, Second Establishment, November 28th, 1776; First Lieutenant, Captain Bond's company, ditto, February 17th, 1777; retired September 26th, 1780; also First Lieutenant, militia.

Norcross, William.   Ensign, Captain Bloomfield's company, Third Battalion, First Establishment; Quartermaster, ditto, February 10th, 1776; Second Lieutenant, Captain Mott's company, Third Battalion, Second Establishment, November 29th, 1776; First Lieutenant, ditto; retired September 26th, 1780.

Parrot, William.   Ensign, Captain Shute's company, Second Battalion, First Establishment, November 28th, 1775; Second Lieutenant, Captain Shaw's company, Second Battalion, Second Establishment, November 29th, 1776; First Lieutenant, Captain Stout's company, ditto, February 5th, 1777; retired September 26th, 1780.

Patterson, Edward. Ensign, Captain Patterson's company, Third Battalion, First Establishment, February 7th, 1776; Second Lieutenant, ditto, October 29th, 1776; Second Lieutenant, Captain Patterson's company, Third Battalion, Second Establishment; First Lieutenant, ditto.

Reading, John. Ensign, Captain Reading's company, Third Battalion, First Establishment; Second Lieutenant, Captain Doughty's company, Third Battalion, Second Establishment; First Lieutenant, Captain Cox's company, ditto, January 1st, 1777; retired September 26th, 1780.

Schenck, Curtenius. First Lieutenant, Captain Longstreet's company, First Battalion, First Establishment, December 16th, 1775; First Lieutenant, Captain M'Mires' company, First Battalion, Second Establishment, November 29th, 1776; retired September 26th, 1780.

Smith, Jeremiah. Second Lieutenant, Captain Shute's company, Second Battalion, First Establishment, November 28th, 1775; First Lieutenant, Captain Dillon's company, Second Battalion, Second Establishment, November 29th, 1776; First Lieutenant, Captain Hollinshead's company, ditto, February 5th, 1777; retired September 26th, 1780.

* Thomas, Edmund D. (Original member.) Private, Captain Bloomfield's company, Third Battalion, First Establishment; cadet, ditto; Ensign, Captain Dickerson's company, ditto, July 19th, 1776; Ensign, Captain Dickerson's company, Third Battalion, Second Establishment, November 29th, 1776; First Lieutenant, ditto, November 11th, 1777; Lieutenant, Third Regiment; Captain by brevet; discharged at the close of the war.

Tuttle, David. Second Lieutenant, Captain Dickerson's company, Third Battalion, First Establishment, February 7th, 1776; First Lieutenant, ditto; discharged with battalion.

SECOND LIEUTENANTS.

Axford, Samuel. Second Lieutenant, Captain Polhemus' company, First Battalion, First Establishment, November 22d, 1775.

Brackenridge, Samuel. Second Lieutenant, Captain Bond's company, Fourth Battalion, Second Establishment, February 17th, 1777; retired September 26th, 1780.

Brewer, Jonathan. Second Lieutenant, Captain Dickerson's company, Third Battalion, Second Establishment, November 29th, 1776; retired September 26th, 1780.

Brown, Daniel. Second Lieutenant, Captain Morris' company, First Battalion, First Establishment, November 8th, 1775.

Clark, Aaron. Second Lieutenant, Eastern Company of Artillery, State Troops; Captain, Company of Artillery, Essex. Officers of this artillery served in General Knox's brigade of artillery during the war.

Cook, George. Second Lieutenant, Fourth Battalion, Second Establishment, November 28th, 1776; retired.

Costigin, Francis. Ensign, Captain Conway's company, First Battalion, First Establishment, November 21st, 1775; Second Lieutenant, Captain M'Mires' company, First Battalion, Second Establishment, November 29th, 1776; retired September 26th, 1780.

Day, Aaron. Ensign, Captain Cox's company, Third Battalion, Second Establishment; Second Lieutenant, ditto, January 1st, 1777; retired September 26th, 1780.

Gaulidet, Edgar. Ensign, Captain Imlay's company, Third Battalion, First Establishment, February 7th, 1776; Second Lieutenant, Captain Gifford's company, Third Battalion, Second Establishment, November 29th, 1776; retired September 26th, 1780.

Hackett, Samuel. Ensign, Captain Doughty's company, Third Battalion, Second Establishment, November 29th, 1776; Second Lieutenant, Captain Cox's company, ditto; retired September 26th, 1780.

Holmes, Elisha. Second Lieutenant, Fourth Battalion, Second Establishment, November 28th, 1776; Second Lieutenant, Captain Holmes' company, ditto, February 17th, 1777; retired September 26th, 1780.

Johnson, Richard. Second Lieutenant, Captain Howell's company, First Battalion, First Establishment, November 14th, 1775.

† Kinney, John. (Original member.) Ensign, Captain Potter's company, Third Battalion, First Establishment, July 19th, 1776; Ensign, Captain Patterson's company, Third Battalion, Second Establishment, November 29th, 1776; Second Lieutenant, ditto; retired September 26th, 1780; Captain by brevet.

Lane, Abraham. Ensign, Captain Longstreet's company, First Battalion, First Establishment, December 16th, 1775; Second Lieutenant, Captain Baldwin's company, First Battalion, Second Establishment, November 29th, 1776; retired September 26th, 1780.

Lawrence, Benjamin. Second Lieutenant, Fourth Battalion, Second Establishment, November 28th, 1776; Second Lieutenant, Captain Pearson's company, ditto, February 17th, 1777; retired September 26th, 1780.

* Pennington, William S. (Original member.) Serjeant, " Lamb's Artillery." (Second Regiment Artillery), Continental Army, March 7th, 1777; Second Lieutenant, ditto, September 12th, 1778; Captain by brevet.

Pierson, Daniel. Second Lieutenant, Captain Imlay's company, Third Battalion, First Establishment, February 7th, 1776; discharged with battalion.

Pipes, John. First Lieutenant, Fourth Battalion, Second Establishment, November 28th, 1776; Second Lieutenant, Captain Wade's company, ditto, February 17th, 1777; retired September 26th, 1780; also First Lieutenant, militia.

Quimby, Josiah. Second Lieutenant, Captain Potter's company, Third Battalion, First Establishment, February 7th, 1776; discharged with battalion.

* Reed, John. (Original member.) Ensign, Captain

Lyon's company, Fourth Battalion, Second Establishment, February 17th, 1777; Second Lieutenant, ditto, October 3d, 1777; retired September 26th, 1780.

Reynolds, George. Ensign, Captain Shaw's company, Second Battalion, First Establishment, December 25th, 1775; Ensign, Captain Brearley's company, Second Battalion, Second Establishment, November 29th, 1776; Second Lieutenant, Captain Luce's company, ditto, February 5th, 1777; retired September 26th, 1780; also Captain, militia.

Ross, George. Ensign, Captain Meeker's Company, First Battalion, First Establishment, December 10th, 1775; Second Lieutenant, Captain Anderson's company, Second Battalion, Second Establishment; Second Lieutenant, Captain Reading's company, ditto, February 5th, 1777; retired September 26th, 1780.

Ryerson, Thomas. Ensign, Captain Brearley's company, Second Battalion, First Establishment, November 20th, 1775; Second Lieutenant, Captain Scott's company, ditto, July 18th, 1776; Second Lieutenant, Captain Shute's company, Second Battalion, Second Establishment, November 29th, 1776; prisoner of war; retired February 5th, 1777.

Shinn, Buddle. Quartermaster, Second Battalion, First Establishment, November 27th, 1775; declined; Second Lieutenant, Captain Rosecrantz's company, Third Battalion, Second Establishment, November 29th, 1776; retired September 26th, 1780.

Sickles, Thomas. Ensign, Captain Polhemus' company, First Battalion, First Establishment, November 22d, 1775; Second Lieutenant, Captain Piatt's company, First Battalion, Second Establishment, November 29th, 1776; retired September 26th, 1780.

Woodruff, Lewis. Second Lieutenant, Fourth Battalion, Second Establishment, November 28th, 1776; retired February 17th, 1777.

Wright, Nathan. Second Lieutenant, Fourth Battalion, Second Establishment; retired.

ENSIGNS.

Anderson, William. Ensign, Captain Bond's company, Fourth Battalion, Second Establishment, February 17th, 1777; Ensign, First Regiment, June 21st, 1781; discharged at the close of the war.

Axtell, Ebenezer. Ensign, Captain Conway's company, First Battalion, Second Establishment, November 29th, 1776; retired September 26th, 1780.

Bankson, Andrew. Ensign, Captain Lawrie's company, Second Battalion, First Establishment, September 5th, 1776; Ensign, Captain Stout's company, Second Battalion, Second Establishment, November 29th, 1776; retired February 5th, 1777.

Beatty, ——. Ensign, Captain Pearson's company, Fourth Battalion, Second Establishment, February 17th, 1777; retired September 26th, 1780.

* Bishop, John. (Original member.) Serjeant, First Battalion, Second Establishment; Ensign, ditto, February 1st, 1779; Ensign, First Regiment; discharged at the close of the war.

Bowne, Peter. Serjeant, Captain Kinsey's company, Fourth Battalion, Second Establishment; Ensign, Captain Holmes' company, ditto, February 17th, 1777; retired September 26th, 1780.

* Brooks, Almerin. (Original member.) Serjeant, Second Battalion, Second Establishment, June 9th, 1777; Ensign, ditto, June 17th, 1780; Ensign, Second Regiment; discharged at the close of the war.

Brown, David. Ensign, Second Battalion, Second Establishment, March 11th, 1777; retired September 26th, 1780.

Carter, William. Ensign, Captain Anderson's company, Second Battalion, Second Establishment, November 29th, 1776; retired February 5th, 1777.

Catarich, William. Ensign, Captain Gifford's company, Third Battalion, Second Establishment, November 29th, 1776; retired September 26th, 1780.

Clunn, Matthew. Ensign, Captain Yard's¹ company, Second Battalion, Second Establishment, February 5th, 1777; retired September 26th, 1780.

Cottnam, George. Ensign, Third Battalion, First Establishment, February 29th, 1776; discharged with battalion.

Dare, David. Serjeant, Captain Bloomfield's company, Third Battalion, First Establishment, February 7th, 1776; Ensign, Captain Gordon's company, Third Battalion, Second Establishment, November 29th, 1776; retired September 26th, 1780.

Dennis, Ezekiel. Ensign, Captain Rosecrantz's company, Third Battalion, Second Establishment, November 29th, 1776; retired September 26th, 1780.

Ewing, George. Ensign, Continental Army.

* Faulkner, Peter. (Original member.) Private, " Lee's Legion," Continental Army; Corporal, ditto, April 6th, 1778; Serjeant, ditto, January 1st, 1779; Ensign, Second Regiment, to date June 17th, 1780; discharged at the close of the war.

Fithian, Glover. Ensign, Captain Longstreet's company, First Battalion, Second Establishment, November 29th, 1776; retired September 26th, 1780.

Geary, John. Private, First Battalion, Second Establishment, September 1st, 1777; Ensign, ditto, February 1st, 1779; Ensign, First Regiment; resigned March 28th, 1783.

Harbert, Thomas. Ensign, Captain Piatt's company, First Battalion, Second Establishment, November 29th, 1776; retired September 26th, 1780.

;* Hopper, John. (Original member.) Ensign, Second Regiment, June 21st, 1781; discharged at the close of the war.

Howell, James. Ensign, Captain Yard's company, Second Battalion, Second Establishment, November 29th, 1776; retired February 5th, 1777.

* Hyer, Jacob, Jr. (Original member.) Ensign, Second Regiment, June 27th, 1781; discharged at the close of the war.

Kerr, William. Ensign, Fourth Battalion, Second Establishment, November 28th, 1776; retired February 17th, 1777; also Ensign, militia.

Kinney, Thomas. Private, Third Battalion, First Establishment; Ensign, ditto, July 19th, 1776; discharged with battalion.

Ludlam, Jacob. Ensign, Captain M'Mires' company, First Battalion, Second Establishment, November 29th, 1776; retired September 26th, 1780.

* Luce, Francis. (Original member.) Private, Second Battalion, Second Establishment; Ensign, Second Regiment, to date June 17th, 1780; discharged at the close of the war.

Morris, Jonathan F. Ensign, Captain Morris' company, First Battalion, First Establishment, September 14th, 1776.

Phillips, John. Ensign, Captain Stout's company, Second Battalion, Second Establishment, February 5th, 1777; retired September 26th, 1780.

Reed, John. (Original member.) Serjeant, "Spencer's Regiment," Continental Army, February 1st, 1777; Ensign, ditto, May 12th, 1779; discharged at the close of the war.

Reeves, John. Corporal, Captain Bloomfield's company, Third Battalion, First Establishment; Serjeant, ditto; Ensign, Captain Shaw's company, Second Battalion, Second Establishment, November 29th, 1776; retired February 5th, 1777.

Rue, Lewis. Serjeant, Captain Lawrie's company, Second Battalion, First Establishment; Ensign, Captain Reading's company, Second Battalion, Second Establishment, February 5th, 1777; retired September 26th, 1780.

Salmon, Nathaniel. Ensign, Captain Luce's company, Second Battalion, Second Establishment, February 5th, 1777; retired September 26th, 1780.

Scobey, James. Private, Third Battalion, Second Establishment; Ensign, ditto.

Smith, Thomas. Ensign, Captain Dillon's company, Second Battalion, Second Establishment, November 29th, 1776; retired February 5th, 1777.

* Sprowls, Moses. (Original member.) Private, Third Battalion, First Establishment; private, Captain Patterson's company, Third Battalion, Second Establishment; private, First Regiment; Serjeant, Third Regiment; Quartermaster Serjeant, ditto; Ensign, Second Regiment, June 21st, 1781; Ensign, First Regiment; discharged at the close of the war.

Stewart, ——. Ensign, Captain Kinsey's company, Fourth Battalion, Second Establishment; retired September 26th, 1780.

* Suydam, Cornelius R. (Original member.) Ensign, First Regiment, May 30th, 1782; discharged at the close of the war.

Thompson, Andrew. Serjeant, Captain M'Mires' company, First Battalion, Second Establishment; Ensign, " Spencer's Regiment," Continental Army; also private, militia.

* Tuttle, William. (Original member.) Private, Third Battalion, Second Establishment; Serjeant, ditto, February 1st, 1779; Serjeant, Captain Anderson's company, Third Regiment; Ensign, First Regiment, June 21st, 1781; discharged at the close of the war.

Van Cleve, William. Ensign, Captain Mott's company, Third Battalion, Second Establishment, November 29th, 1776; retired September 26th, 1780.

Vanderventer, Peter. Ensign, Captain Polhemus' company, First Battalion, Second Establishment, November 29th, 1776; retired September 26th, 1780.

Wood, Clement. Ensign, Captain Wade's company, Fourth Battalion, Second Establishment, February 17th, 1777; retired September 26th, 1780.

NOTE.—Men were enlisted for a stated period. Officers were nominated by the Provincial Congress and appointed by the Continental Congress. Some declined, some resigned, some were discharged with the troops, some were retired, but the great majority continued to the end of the war.
* Signed order of September 23, 1783, on John Pierce, Esquire, Paymaster-General to the Army of the United States.
† No record of the deposit of the month's pay.
‡ Never deposited the month's pay.
The one month's pay of Ichabod Burnet deposited by William Burnet, Jr., July, 1793.
The one month's pay of Daniel Baldwin remitted by resolution of the Society on account of his serious wounds and his financial condition.
‖ Signed the copy of the Institution of the Cincinnati headed by the signature of Washington, written on parchment and now in possession of the General Society.
§ Signed Counterpart of the Institution mentioned above, and in possession of the General Society.

Roster of the New Jersey Officers of the Continental Line, Army of the Revolution, Who Died in the Service, or Before the Society Was Organized

MAJOR GENERALS.

Alexander, William (Lord Stirling). Colonel, First Battalion, First Establishment, November 7th, 1775; Brigadier General, Continental Army, March 11th, 1776; Major General, Continental Army, February 19th, 1777; died of gout, at Albany, New York, January 15th, 1783, while in command of the Northern Department; taken prisoner at Bushwick, Long Island, August 27th, 1776; commanded a division of the Continental Army at the battle of Brandywine, corps de reserve at Germantown, and left wing of the army at Monmouth; twice received the thanks of Congress (January 29th, 1776, and September 24th, 1779) for conspicuous services; death announced in Congress, January 28th, 1783.

LIEUTENANT COLONELS.

Barber, Francis. Major, Third Battalion, First Establishment, February 9th, 1776; Lieutenant Colonel, Third Battalion, Second Establishment, November 28th, 1776; Lieutenant Colonel, Third Regiment, to date January 1st, 1777; Lieutenant Colonel Commandant, ditto, January 6th, 1783; killed by a falling tree, in camp, at New Windsor, New York, February 11th, 1783; was sub-Inspector General, staff of General

Steuben, April 1st, 1778; Adjutant General to Major General Lord Stirling; Adjutant General to General Sullivan; Deputy Adjutant to Major General Nathaniel Greene; severely wounded at the battle of Monmouth; wounded at the battle of Newtown, and again at the siege of Yorktown.

MAJORS.

D'Hart, Maurice. Major and Aid-de-Camp to Major General William Irvine; Major and Aid-de-Camp to Brigadier General Anthony Wayne; killed at Fort Lee, New Jersey.

Morris, Joseph. Captain, First Battalion, First Establishment, November 8th, 1775; Captain, First Battalion, Second Establishment, November 29th, 1776; Major, ditto; severely wounded at the battle of Germantown, October 4th, 1777; and died January 7th, 1778.

Piatt, Daniel. Captain, First Battalion, First Establishment, December 16th, 1775; Captain, First Battalion, Second Establishment, November 29th, 1776; Major, First Regiment, to date January 4th, 1778; died of disease at camp near Morristown, April 16th, 1780.

Witherspoon, James. Brigade Major, with rank of Major, staff of Brigadier General William Maxwell; killed by cannon shot, in the streets of Germantown, October 4th, 1777.

ADJUTANTS.

Clough, Alexander. Second Lieutenant, Captain M'Mires' company, First Battalion, First Establishment, December 15th, 1775; Adjutant, First Battalion, First Establishment, to date December 15th, 1775; Adjutant, First Battalion, Second Establishment, November 28th, 1776; died in service, December, 1778.

SURGEONS.

Horton, Jonathan. Surgeon in General Hospital; died March, 1780; also Surgeon, militia.

Howell, Lewis. Surgeon, Second Battalion, Second Establishment, November 28th, 1776; resigned July 5th, 1778. (New Jersey Cincinnati record. Died June 29th, 1778.)

CHAPLAINS.

Caldwell, James. Chaplain, Third Battalion, First Establishment, February 9th, 1776; discharged with battalion; afterwards Deputy Quartermaster and Assistant Commissary General, Continental Army. (See Assistant Quartermaster Generals, militia.) Murdered at Elizabethport, New Jersey, November 24th, 1781.

CAPTAINS.

Anderson, Ephraim. Second Lieutenant, Captain Stout's company, Second Battalion, First Establishment, December 18th, 1775; Adjutant, ditto; Captain, Second Battalion, Second Establishment, November 29th, 1776; died in service; also Major, militia.

Dallas, Archibald. Second Lieutenant, Captain Meeker's company, First Battalion, First Establishment, December 9, 1775; Second Lieutenant, Captain Howell's company, First Battalion, Second Establishment, November 29th, 1776; Captain, Fourth Battalion, Second Establishment; Captain, "Spencer's Regiment," Continental Army; killed in action, January 28th, 1779; also Captain, militia.

Faulkner, William. Captain, Second Battalion, First Establishment, November 13th, 1775; died April 25th, 1776.

Lawrie, James. Captain, Second Battalion, First Establishment, November 27th, 1775; Captain, Second Battalion, Second Establishment, November 29th, 1776; taken prisoner; died while prisoner of war.

M'Mires, Andrew. Captain, First Battalion, First Establishment, December 15th, 1775; Captain, First Battalion, Second Establishment, November 29th, 1776; killed at the battle of Germantown, October 4th, 1777.

Neil, Daniel. Captain-Lieutenant, Eastern Company of Artillery, State Troops, March 1st, 1776; Captain, ditto; killed at the battle of Princeton, January 3d, 1777. Officers of this Artillery served in General Knox's brigade of artillery during the war.

Scott, John B. Captain, Second Battalion, First Establishment, December 9th, 1775; died in service.

Stout, Joseph. Captain, Second Battalion, First Establishment, December 18th, 1775; Captain, Second Battalion, Second Establishment, November 29th, 1776; killed at the battle of Brandywine, September 11th, 1777.

Voorhies, Peter V. Second Lieutenant, Captain Conway's company, First Battalion, First Establishment, November 29th, 1775; First Lieutenant, ditto, September 18th, 1776; First Lieutenant, Captain Longstreet's company, First Battalion, Second Establishment, November 29th, 1776; Captain, ditto, November 1st, 1777; Captain, First Regiment; taken prisoner and murdered by Tories, near New Brunswick, October 26th, 1779.

LIEUTENANTS.

Hays, Thomas. Lieutenant, Continental Army; died in service; also Lieutenant, militia.

Hurley, James. Lieutenant, Continental Army; died in service.

FIRST LIEUTENANTS.

Jenkins, Nathaniel. Second Lieutenant, Captain Cumming's company, Second Battalion, Second Establishment, February 5th, 1777; First Lieutenant, ditto, January 1st, 1778; Ensign, Second Regiment; died April 5th, 1779.

Peck, Constant. First Lieutenant, Third Battalion, First Establishment, February 24th, 1776; died April 9th, 1776.

SECOND LIEUTENANTS.

Ashman, James. Second Lieutenant, Captain Lawrie's company, Second Battalion, First Establishment, November 27th, 1775; died September 11th, 1776.

Higgins, John. Second Lieutenant, Captain Scott's company, Second Battalion, First Establishment, December 9th, 1775; died July 12th, 1776.

ENSIGNS.

Hurley, Martin. Private, Captain M'Mires' company, First Battalion, First Establishment; Serjeant, ditto, December 25th, 1775; Ensign, First Battalion, Second Establishment; killed at the battle of Germantown, October 4th, 1777.

McFarland, George. Ensign, Fourth Battalion, Second Establishment, November 28th, 1776; died December, 1776; also Ensign, militia.

Ogden, Moses. Private, "Spencer's Regiment," Continental Army; Serjeant, ditto, October 1st, 1777; Ensign, ditto, May 12th, 1779; killed.

Rodgers, James. Serjeant, Fourth Battalion, Second Establishment, March 1st, 1777; Ensign, Third Regiment, to date February 1st, 1779; killed in action at Springfield, New Jersey, August 24th, 1780.

Sprowls, James. Ensign, Captain Bond's company, Fourth Battalion, Second Establishment; died June 26th, 1777.

Copy of Warrant Signed at Princeton, N. J., September 23rd, 1783

To John Pierce, Esqr.,
    Pay Master Genl, to the Army of the U. States.

Sir:—

    Please to pay Major Rich,d Cox, Treasurer of the N. J. State Association of the Cincinnati, or his order one months pay of our several grades respectively, and deduct the same from the ballance which shall be found due us at the final liquidation of our accounts, for which this shall be your warrant.

Elias Dayton, B, Genl
Rich,d Cox Major
Alex,r Mitchell Capt.
John Holmes Capt,
Samuel Hendry Capt
Jonathan Dayton Capt
Aaron Ogdon Capt
Able Weyman Capt
Jeremiah Ballard Capt
Jonathan Holmes Capt
Nath,l Leonard Capt
Cyrus D. Hart Capt
Ebenr Elmer Surgeon
Jacob Harris Surgeon
Moses G. Elmer Surg,n Mate
Wm Pennington Lieut 2nd Reg,t
  Artillery
Luther Halsey Lieut
Ab,m Appleton Lieut
Edmund D. Thomas Lieut
Benajah Osman Lieut
Joseph Buck Lieut
Sam.l M. Shute Lt.
Sam.l Seely Lt.
·Sam.l Conn Lt.
John Rucastle Lt.
George Walker Lt.
Absalom Bonham Lt.
Will,m Kersey Lt.
Eph,m Whitlock Lt.
Eden Burrows Lt
Wessel T. Stout Lt
John Reed Lt
John Blair Lt
John Bishop Ens,n

Moses Sproul do
Wm Tuttle do
Wm Shute do
Almarine Brooks do
Israel Shreeve Col.
Jno N. Cumming Lt. Col. Com,dr.
Nath,l Bowman Major 2nd Reg,t
Jno Burrows Major Col. Spencers
Derrick Lane Capt 2nd Reg,t
Wm Helms Capt 2nd do
Jno Peck Lt do
Jabez Campfield Surg,n Dragoons
Jeremiah Bruen Major of Artificers
Abram Stout Late Lt 2nd, Reg,t
John Heard Capt P. L. D.
Jon,h Forman Lt Col.
Wm Barton Capt
M. Ogden Col. .
Jonathan Phillips Late Capt
Jonathan Rhea Lieut
Wm Piatt Capt
Sam.l Reading Major
James Heard Capt P Legion
F. Luce Ensign
Jacob Hyer Ensign
Abraham Kinney Lt 2nd Regt
  Dragoons
Oliver Spencer Colonel
Cap D Hart
Capt Howell
Capt Morton
Peter Faulkner Ens.r
Jno Hooper do
C. R. Suydam do

Copy of Richard Cox, Treasurers Account With John Pierce, Esq., Pay-master to the Army of the United States

Dr. John Pierce Esq,r Pay Master Genl,l
    To the Treasurer of the Cincinnati Society of N. Jersey

	To B Genl Dayton order in favor of society for		120.
	To Major Rich,d Cox	do	50.
	To Capt Alex Mitchell	do	40.
	To Capt John Holmes	do	40.
	To Capt Samuel Hendry	do	40.
	To Capt Jonathan Dayton	do	40.
	To Capt Aaron Ogden	do	40.
	To Capt Able Weyman	do	40.
	To Capt Jeremiah Ballard	do	40.
	To Capt Jonathan Holmes	do	40.
	To Capt Nath,l Leonard	do	40.
	To Capt Cyrus D Hart	do	40.
	To Lieut Luther Halsey	do	26.60
	To Lieut Abram Appleton	do	26.60
	To Edmund D. Thomas	do	26.60
	To — Benajah Osman	do	26.60
	To — Joseph Buck	do	26.60
	To Sam.l Shute	do	26.60
	To Sam.l Seely	do	26.60
	To — Sam,l Conn	do	26.60
	To — John Rucastle	do	26.60
	To — George Walker	do	26.60
	To — Absolem Bonham	do	26.60
	To — Wm Kersey	do	26.60
	To — Ephraim Whitlock	do	26.60
	To — Eden Burrows	do	26.60
	To — Wessel Stout	do	26.60
	To — Jno Reed	do	26.60
	To — Jno Blair	do	26.60
	To Ensign Jno Bishop	do	20.
	To — Moses Sproul	do	20.
	To — William Tuttle	do	20.
	To — Wm Shute	do	20
	To — Almarine Brooks	do	20
	To Eben.r Elmer Surgeon	do	
	To Jacob Harris do	do	
Recd none	To Moses G. Elmer Mate	do	
	To Wm. Pennington Lieut Artillery	do	33.30
	To Col Israel Shreve	do	75.
	To Lt Col Com, dr Jno N Cummings	do	75.
	To Major Nath,l Bowman	do	·50.
	To Major Jno Burrows	do	50.
	To Capt Derrick Lane	do	40.
	To — Wm Helmes	do	40.
	To Lieut Jno Peck	do	26.60
Recd none	To Jabez Campfield Surgeon Dragoons	do	
Recd none	To Jeremiah Bruen Major of Artificers	do	
	To Lieut Abram Stout	do	26.60
	To Jno Heard Capt P. Light Dragoons	do	50.
	To Lieut Col Jonathan Forman	do	60
	To Capt Wm Barton	do	40.
	To Col. Matthias Ogden	do	75
	To Capt Jonathan Phillips	do	40.
	To Jonathan Rhea Lieut	do	26.60
	To Capt Wm Piatt	do	40.
	To Major Sam,l Reading	do	50.
	To Capt James Heard P. Legion	do	50.
	To Ensign Francis Luce	do	20.
	To — Jacob Hyer	do	20.
Recd none	To Abram Kinney Lt Lt. Dragoons	do	
	To Col Oliver Spencer	do	75.
	To Capt Jno Howell	do	40.
	To Capt Absolem Martin	do	40.
	To Ensign Peter Faulkner	do	20.
	To — Jno Hopper	do	20.
	To — Cornelius R. Sydam	do	20.

A List of the Members of the Society of the Cincinnati, in the State of New Jersey, Made by Richard Cox, Treasurer, July, 1788

No.	Names	Rank	Remarks
1	Elias Dayton	Brig. Genl.	
	Matthias Ogden	" "	
	David Forman	" "	
	Israel Shreve	Colonel	
5	Oliver Spencer	"	
	John Noble Cumming	"	
	David Brearly	Lieut. Colonel	
	Jonathan Forman	" "	
	Richard Howell	Major	
10	Joseph Bloomfield †	"	Deposited no pay
	John Ross	"	
	John Burrows	"	
	John Hollinshead †	"	Deposited no pay
	Samuel Reading	"	
15	Richard Cox	"	
	Nathaniel Donnall	"	Never met the Society
Dead †	Nathanial Bowman	"	Never met the Society
	Jeremiah Bruen	"	Deposited no pay
	Richard Lloyd †	"	Ditto
20	John Heard	Captain	
	James Heard	"	
	Jeremiah Ballard	Captain	
	Giles Mead	"	
	† Alexander Mitchell ‡	"	Never met the Society
			—not to be paid
25	William Helmes	Major	
	John Holmes	" Capt	
	Aaron Ogden	" Capt	
	Samuel Hendry	" Capt	
	William Piatt	" Capt	
30	Jonathan Dayton	" Capt	
	Jonathan Holmes	"	Never met the Society.
			Capt.
	Cyrus D. Hart	"	Ditto Capt.
	Nathaniel Leonard	"	Capt.
	John Howell	Captain	
35	William Barton	"	
	Absolom Martin	"	Never met the Society
	Derick Lane	"	Removed to the State
			of New York
	John Polhemus	"	
	Jonathan Phillips	"	
40	Jacob Piatt †	"	Deposited no pay
	Luther Halsey	"	
	Edmond D. Thomas	"	
	Abraham Appleton	"	
	John Blair	"	Removed out of the State
45	Ephraim Whitlock	"	* Never met the Society
	Eden Burrows	"	Removed out of the State
	John Reed	"	
	John Ruecastle	"	*Removed out of the State
	Samuel Seely	"	* Never met the Society
50	Absolom Bonham	"	Never met the Society

No.	Names	Rank	Remarks
	William Kersey	Captain	
	Samuel M. Shute	Lieut.	
	Jonathan Rhea	"	
	John Peck	"	Removed out of the State
55	Banajah Osman	"	
	Joseph Buck	"	Never met the Society
	Wessel Tenbrook Stout	"	
	William Pennington	"	
	Chillion Ford	"	
60	Jonathan Snowden	"	Deposited no pay
	James Anderson	Capt. Lieut.	Ditto
	James Bonnell	Captain	Never met the Society
	Robert Pemberton	Lieut.	Ditto
	Seth Bowen	Capt. Lieut.	Ditto
65	Eli Elmer	Lieut.	
	John Shreve*	"	* Never met the Society or deposited any pay
	Anthony Reckless	"	* Ditto Never met the Society
	George Walker	"	Removed out of the State
	Abraham Kinney	"	* Ditto Deposited no pay
70	John Bishop	Ensign	Never met the Society
	William Shute	"	
	Peter Faulkner	"	Never met the Society
	Almarine Brooks	"	
	Francis Luce	"	
75	Moses Sprowls	"	
	William Tuttle	"	* Never met the Society
	John Hopper	"	
	Jacob Hyer	"	
	Cornelius R. Sydam	"	Never met the Society
80	John Read	"	Never met the Society
	Ephraim Darby	Lieut.	
	Rev. Andrew Hunter	Chaplain	
	Lewis Dunham	Surgeon	
	Jazeb Campfield	"	
85	George Campble	"	
	Ebenezar Elmer	"	
	Jacob Harris	"	Never met the Society
	John Conway	Lieut. Col.	* Ditto Ent. this State Society 5th July 1788
	Elias Boudinott, Esq.	Honoary	
90	Thomas Henderson, Esq.	"	
	Robert Lettis Hooper, Esq.	"	
	John Beaty, Esq.	Comm. of Prisoners	
	Able Weyman	Capt	Dead
	Samuel Conn	"	"
95	Abraham Stout	Lieut.	Never met the Society
	Frederick Frelinghuysen, Esq.	Honoary	
	Daniel Baldwin	Capt	
	Moses Elmer	Surg. Mate	
	William Burnet	Surgeon	
100	James F. Armstrong	Chaplain	
	James Giles	Capt. Lieut.	
	Ebenezar Stockton	Surgeon	

* Pen drawn through this where underlined.
† July 6, 1791, the Treasurer in his account charges himself as follows, to wit: To cash received of Major Bloomfield for four years' interest which he received on a certificate deposited for one month's pay, $12.
† The one month's pay of John Hollinshead, deposited 1789.
† Ditto. Richard Lloyd, deposited 1796 by his successor, William Lloyd.
† Ditto. Jacob Piatt, deposited 1789.
‡ Alexander Mitchell dropped from roll September, 1783.
† These marks *preceding* names appear so on list in writing of Richard Cox.

49